BARKER CREEK®

Adjectives

Text and Illustration
Copyright © 2016
by Barker Creek Publishing, Inc.

Graphic Designer:
Vickie Spurgin

Printed in the USA

ISBN: 978-1-928961-15-4
Item Number: 1604

BARKER CREEK®
Lifestyle Products for Office, School, and Home

P.O. Box 2610
Poulsbo, WA 98730
www.barkercreek.com
800.692.5833

Adj...
Activ...

A Reading FUNdamentals™ Book

Other books in this series include:

Homophones, Synonyms & Antonyms Activity Book

Compound Words Activity Book

Nouns Activity Book

Verbs & Adverbs Activity Book

Collective Nouns Activity Book

Prefixes/Suffixes Activity Book

Idioms Activity Book

Similes Activity Book

Also Available from Barker Creek:

Grammar Poster Set

All of the titles in our Reading FUNdamentals™ series are also available as E-Books.

Visit us at www.barkercreek.com for more information.

Adjective

a word that describes or modifies the meaning of a noun or pronoun

( ) **playful, imaginative** | *children*

lovable, big | *dog* ( )

( ) **cozy, brick** | *house*

wide-eyed, green | *frog* ( )

( ) **fierce, young** | *lion*

warm, sunny | *day* ( )

( ) **endearing, elderly** | *friend*

Table of Contents

How to Use This Book

Please read this entire page before getting started.

There are 19 adjective lessons in this book. You may choose to use these lessons to introduce adjectives or simply for a review.

For the older students, you may also want to discuss **possessive**, **demonstrative**, **interrogative** and **indefinite** adjectives. These types of adjectives are not addressed in this book, but may be introduced as you are working through the lessons.

Page Set Up

1. Check the plans!
Study the picture. What things do you see? Look for all of the details in the illustration.

2. Plug it in!
Write six adjectives in the six boxes that describe the picture. You may want to use a thesaurus for finding more adjectives.

*(**Note:** Because the picture has not been colored, the students will not be able to use color words as adjectives.)*

3. Dig in!
Write three sentences about the picture using the six adjectives. Then, color the picture.

4. Plan the design!
*(**Note:** The story provided is for the teacher to read aloud to the students. The story should be read once, all the way through, while the students **listen**. After the story has been read once, in its entirety, read again, **stopping at each star (★)** found in the story. Allow time for the children to **draw what they just heard**.)*

Each student will need a large piece of paper and a pencil. Some of the stories will require crayons and scissors. Read the story first to determine the supplies needed.

5. In the spotlight!
Use a highlighter, a yellow crayon or marker to identify at least five adjectives. Then, with a pencil, circle the nouns that each adjective describes.

6. Tack it on!
These activities are fun extensions that may be done in the classroom or used at home.

Blank Page Templates

Templates are provided on pages 46-47. These are provided so that you can create your own adjective lessons.

More Adjectives

On pages 48-49 you will find a list of more adjectives. These may be used for creating more adjective activities. Also reproduce these for each child to use as a reference for future story writing. These words may also be used with the **Adjective Fun Sheet** on page 50.

Adjective Fun Sheet

Provided on page 50 is a fun activity. This is a time for the students to think outside of the box! You will need to make a few copies of the adjectives list from pages 48-49. These should be cut out and placed in a bowl, hat, or some type of container. The students should close their eyes and choose two adjectives. These words will be used for the activity.

Example:
A student chooses the adjectives **shiny** and **green**.

> Here is something **shiny** and **green**.
> It is a nickel lying in the grass.

(The student then may illustrate the sometimes silly and sometimes clever sentence.) Allow your students to do this frequently, giving them the opportunity to be creative!

Review Test

Measure what your students have learned about adjectives. Refer to the tests on pages 46 and 47.

Answer Key

TEST 1
1. charming, young
2. fast, jolly
3. hungry, cool
4. tight, new
5. tall, plain
6. gorgeous, yellow
7. small, shiny
8. sharp, delicious
9. round, green
10. icy, sunny

TEST 2
1. loud, football, big
2. speeding, rocky
3. five, yellow, tall
4. fire-breathing, lovely
5. funny, little, big
6. delicious, cherry
7. tiny, yellow
8. big, hot, shining
9. eight, orange, my, grandma's, front
10. wool, striped, dirty

What is an Adjective?

A word that describes a noun or pronoun

Name: _____

Looking for Adjectives

Check the plans!

Study it!

What things do you see? Look for ALL of the details in the illustration.

Plug it in!

Think about it and write it!

Can you think of **six adjectives** that describe the picture above? You may need to use a thesaurus.

❶

❷

❸

❹

❺

❻

Dig in!

Write three sentences about the picture above using the six adjectives.

Color the picture.

❶ _____

_____

❷ _____

_____

❸ _____

_____

Reading FUNdamentals™ — Adjectives ©2016 www.barkercreek.com

Plan the Design

Listen to the details of the story carefully!

On a separate piece of paper, draw what you hear as it is being read aloud to you.

In the Spotlight!

Highlight it!
Circle it!

Use a highlighter to identify **at least five adjectives**.

Then, with a pencil, **circle the noun** it describes.

My Special Quilt

On Wednesdays, my grandma and her friends used to get together to visit and do a little quilting. That's when they sew patches of various types of material together to make a unique covering. When I turned 16, my grandma gave me my very own quilt. I still have it 20 years later. Here's what it looks like.

The quilt has 16 patchwork squares. There are four rows with four squares in each row. ★ In the seventh square, she cross-stitched my name in all capital letters, SARAH. ★ In the eighth square, my birthday is cross-stitched, October 4. ★ In two of the squares, there are red hearts. ★ Four of the squares are yellow and purple polka-dot. ★ Three of the squares are my favorite color, green. ★ Dog-printed material covers one of the patches, while fish-printed material covers another. She used this fabric because I had a dog named Biscuit and a fish named Sam. ★ The other three squares are made from multi-colored striped material. This particular cloth was from my favorite pair of pajamas. ★ I really love this quilt!

Tack it on!

Extend It!

What would your special quilt look like? Design one. Write a descriptive paragraph about *your* special quilt.

Name: _____

Looking for Adjectives

Plug it in!

Think about it and write it!

Can you think of **six adjectives** that describe the picture above? You may need to use a thesaurus.

❶ _____   **❹** _____

❷ _____   **❺** _____

❸ _____   **❻** _____

Dig in!

Write three sentences about the picture above using the six adjectives.

Color the picture.

❶ _____

_____

❷ _____

_____

❸ _____

_____

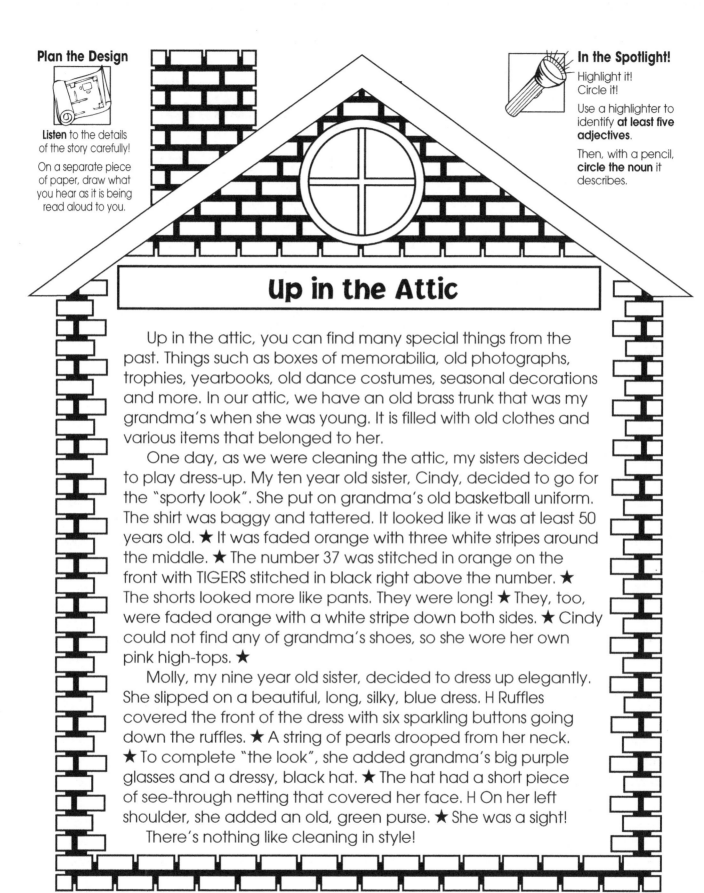

Listen to the details of the story carefully!

On a separate piece of paper, draw what you hear as it is being read aloud to you.

In the Spotlight!

Highlight it!
Circle it!

Use a highlighter to identify **at least five adjectives**.

Then, with a pencil, **circle the noun** it describes.

Up in the Attic

Up in the attic, you can find many special things from the past. Things such as boxes of memorabilia, old photographs, trophies, yearbooks, old dance costumes, seasonal decorations and more. In our attic, we have an old brass trunk that was my grandma's when she was young. It is filled with old clothes and various items that belonged to her.

One day, as we were cleaning the attic, my sisters decided to play dress-up. My ten year old sister, Cindy, decided to go for the "sporty look". She put on grandma's old basketball uniform. The shirt was baggy and tattered. It looked like it was at least 50 years old. ★ It was faded orange with three white stripes around the middle. ★ The number 37 was stitched in orange on the front with TIGERS stitched in black right above the number. ★ The shorts looked more like pants. They were long! ★ They, too, were faded orange with a white stripe down both sides. ★ Cindy could not find any of grandma's shoes, so she wore her own pink high-tops. ★

Molly, my nine year old sister, decided to dress up elegantly. She slipped on a beautiful, long, silky, blue dress. H Ruffles covered the front of the dress with six sparkling buttons going down the ruffles. ★ A string of pearls drooped from her neck. ★ To complete "the look", she added grandma's big purple glasses and a dressy, black hat. ★ The hat had a short piece of see-through netting that covered her face. H On her left shoulder, she added an old, green purse. ★ She was a sight!

There's nothing like cleaning in style!

List eight things that you might find in an attic. Next to each of the eight words, write two adjectives that could be used to describe that particular item.

Name: _____

Looking for Adjectives

Check the plans!

Study it!

What things do you see? Look for ALL of the details in the illustration.

Plug it in!

Think about it and write it!

Can you think of **six adjectives** that describe the picture above? You may need to use a thesaurus.

❶ _____   ❹ _____

❷ _____   ❺ _____

❸ _____   ❻ _____

Dig in!

Write three sentences about the picture above using the six adjectives.

Color the picture.

❶ _____

_____

❷ _____

_____

❸ _____

_____

Plan the Design

Listen to the details of the story carefully!

On a separate piece of paper, draw what you hear as it is being read aloud to you.

Oh! Mr. Sun

Have you ever heard the song: "Oh, Mr. Sun"? I wonder, if the sun were a mister, what would he look like?

Of course, he would be very large, round and a yellow-orange color. ★ He might have bright red, fire-like beams shining out from his head. ★ He would even wear a pair of black sunglasses, just to keep him looking "cool". ★ His arms and legs might look like sizzling, silver sparklers, the kind of fireworks that do not make a loud sound, but only shine and sparkle! ★ His hands and feet would be star-shaped and definitely red in color. ★

On rainy days when he does not come out, he would probably wear a blue baseball cap with the capital letter "P" on it, representing the *Phoenix Suns* basketball team. ★ He might even use an umbrella. ★ He would most certainly shine! I wonder what Mrs. Sun would look like?

Tack it on!

Extend It!

Draw a picture of what you think Mrs. Sun would look like. Write a descriptive paragraph about her.

Name: _____

Looking for Adjectives

Check the plans!

Study it!

What things do you see? Look for ALL of the details in the illustration.

Plug it in!

Think about it and write it!

Can you think of **six adjectives** that describe the picture above? You may need to use a thesaurus.

❶ _____   ❹ _____

❷ _____   ❺ _____

❸ _____   ❻ _____

Dig in!

Write three sentences about the picture above using the six adjectives.

Color the picture.

❶ _____

_____

❷ _____

_____

❸ _____

_____

Plan the Design

Listen to the details of the story carefully!

On a separate piece of paper, draw what you hear as it is being read aloud to you.

In the Spotlight!

Highlight it!
Circle it!

Use a highlighter to identify **at least five adjectives**.

Then, with a pencil, **circle the noun** it describes.

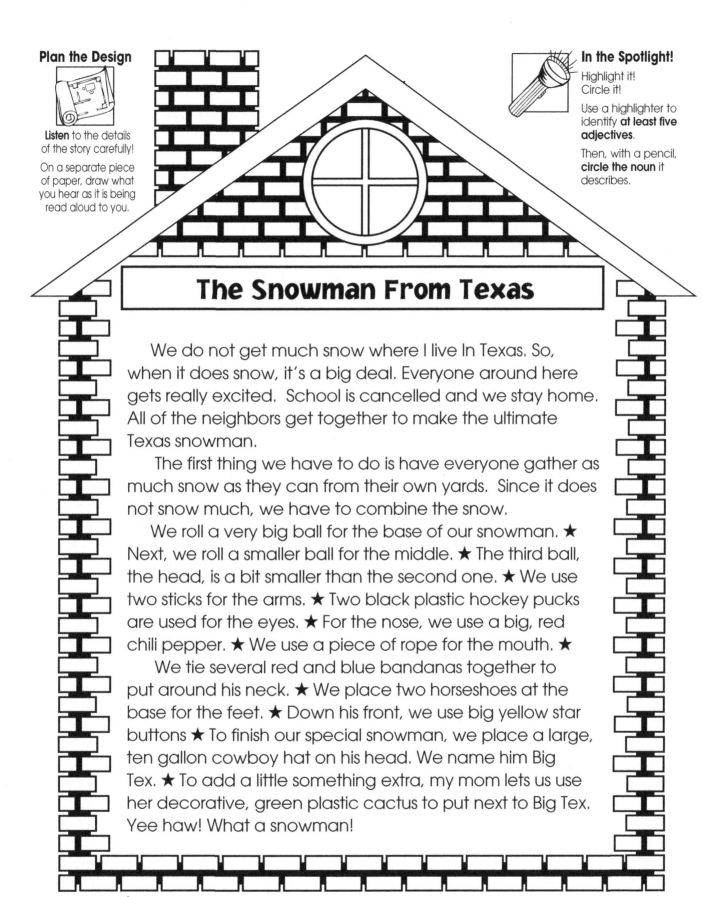

The Snowman From Texas

We do not get much snow where I live In Texas. So, when it does snow, it's a big deal. Everyone around here gets really excited. School is cancelled and we stay home. All of the neighbors get together to make the ultimate Texas snowman.

The first thing we have to do is have everyone gather as much snow as they can from their own yards. Since it does not snow much, we have to combine the snow.

We roll a very big ball for the base of our snowman. ★ Next, we roll a smaller ball for the middle. ★ The third ball, the head, is a bit smaller than the second one. ★ We use two sticks for the arms. ★ Two black plastic hockey pucks are used for the eyes. ★ For the nose, we use a big, red chili pepper. ★ We use a piece of rope for the mouth. ★

We tie several red and blue bandanas together to put around his neck. ★ We place two horseshoes at the base for the feet. ★ Down his front, we use big yellow star buttons ★ To finish our special snowman, we place a large, ten gallon cowboy hat on his head. We name him Big Tex. ★ To add a little something extra, my mom lets us use her decorative, green plastic cactus to put next to Big Tex. Yee haw! What a snowman!

Tack it on!

Extend It!

Where do you live? Draw a snowman that is representative of your state. What items would you use to make your snowman special? **NOTE**: If you live in Texas, draw a partner snowgirl for Big Tex. What special things did you include?

Name: _____

Looking for Adjectives

- -

Plug it in!

Think about it and write it!

Can you think of **six adjectives** that describe the picture above? You may need to use a thesaurus.

❶ _____   ❹ _____

❷ _____   ❺ _____

❸ _____   ❻ _____

- -

Dig in!

Write three sentences about the picture above using the six adjectives.

Color the picture.

❶ _____

_____

❷ _____

_____

❸ _____

_____

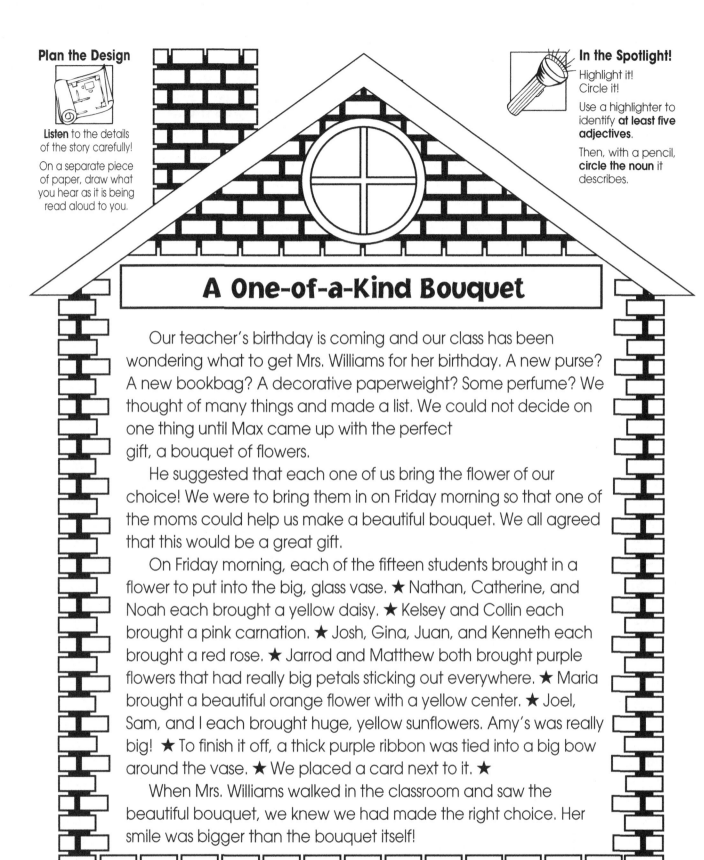

Plan the Design

Listen to the details of the story carefully!

On a separate piece of paper, draw what you hear as it is being read aloud to you.

In the Spotlight!

Highlight it!
Circle it!

Use a highlighter to identify **at least five adjectives**.

Then, with a pencil, **circle the noun** it describes.

A One-of-a-Kind Bouquet

Our teacher's birthday is coming and our class has been wondering what to get Mrs. Williams for her birthday. A new purse? A new bookbag? A decorative paperweight? Some perfume? We thought of many things and made a list. We could not decide on one thing until Max came up with the perfect gift, a bouquet of flowers.

He suggested that each one of us bring the flower of our choice! We were to bring them in on Friday morning so that one of the moms could help us make a beautiful bouquet. We all agreed that this would be a great gift.

On Friday morning, each of the fifteen students brought in a flower to put into the big, glass vase. ★ Nathan, Catherine, and Noah each brought a yellow daisy. ★ Kelsey and Collin each brought a pink carnation. ★ Josh, Gina, Juan, and Kenneth each brought a red rose. ★ Jarrod and Matthew both brought purple flowers that had really big petals sticking out everywhere. ★ Maria brought a beautiful orange flower with a yellow center. ★ Joel, Sam, and I each brought huge, yellow sunflowers. Amy's was really big! ★ To finish it off, a thick purple ribbon was tied into a big bow around the vase. ★ We placed a card next to it. ★

When Mrs. Williams walked in the classroom and saw the beautiful bouquet, we knew we had made the right choice. Her smile was bigger than the bouquet itself!

Tack it on!

Extend It!

Make a bouquet using various materials such as watercolors, colored tissue paper, felt, buttons, pipe cleaners, etc. After designing it, write a descriptive paragraph about it. Be sure and give it to someone special!

Name: _____

Looking for Adjectives

Check the plans!

Study it!
What things do you see? Look for ALL of the details in the illustration.

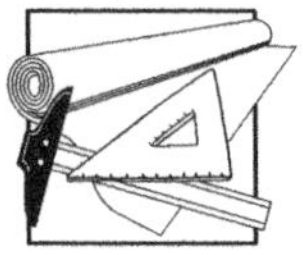

. . . .

Plug it in!

Think about it and write it!

Can you think of **six adjectives** that describe the picture above? You may need to use a thesaurus.

❶ _____   ❹ _____

❷ _____   ❺ _____

❸ _____   ❻ _____

. . . .

Dig in!

Write three sentences about the picture above using the six adjectives.

Color the picture.

❶ _____

_____

❷ _____

_____

❸ _____

_____

Plan the Design

Listen to the details of the story carefully!

On a separate piece of paper, draw what you hear as it is being read aloud to you.

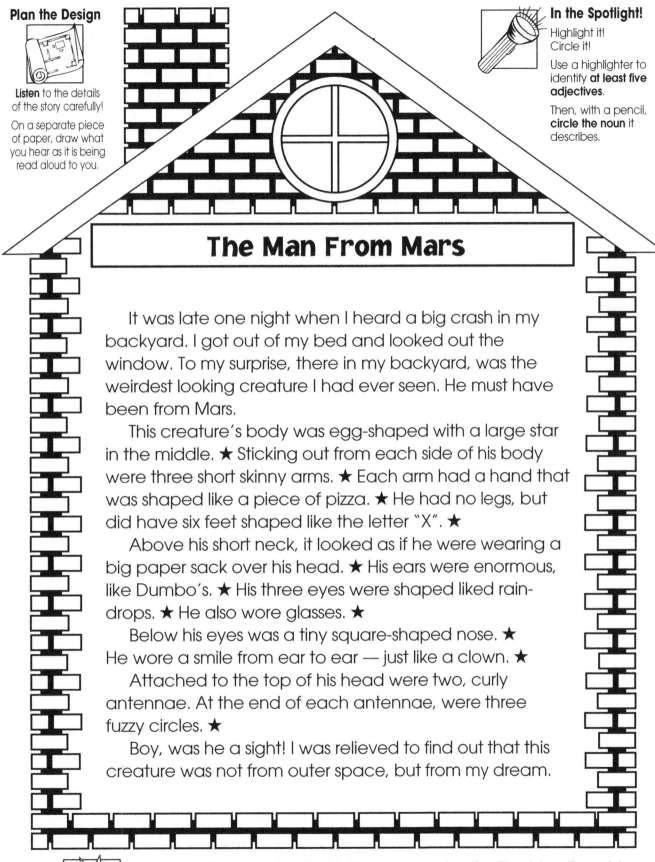

The Man From Mars

It was late one night when I heard a big crash in my backyard. I got out of my bed and looked out the window. To my surprise, there in my backyard, was the weirdest looking creature I had ever seen. He must have been from Mars.

This creature's body was egg-shaped with a large star in the middle. ★ Sticking out from each side of his body were three short skinny arms. ★ Each arm had a hand that was shaped like a piece of pizza. ★ He had no legs, but did have six feet shaped like the letter "X". ★

Above his short neck, it looked as if he were wearing a big paper sack over his head. ★ His ears were enormous, like Dumbo's. ★ His three eyes were shaped liked rain-drops. ★ He also wore glasses. ★

Below his eyes was a tiny square-shaped nose. ★ He wore a smile from ear to ear — just like a clown. ★

Attached to the top of his head were two, curly antennae. At the end of each antennae, were three fuzzy circles. ★

Boy, was he a sight! I was relieved to find out that this creature was not from outer space, but from my dream.

Tack it on!

Extend It!

Have each student write his/her own version for *The Man From Mars*. Divide them into pairs. Let one student read his/her paragraph while the other draws.

Name: _____

Looking for Adjectives

Check the plans!

Study it!

What things do you see? Look for ALL of the details in the illustration.

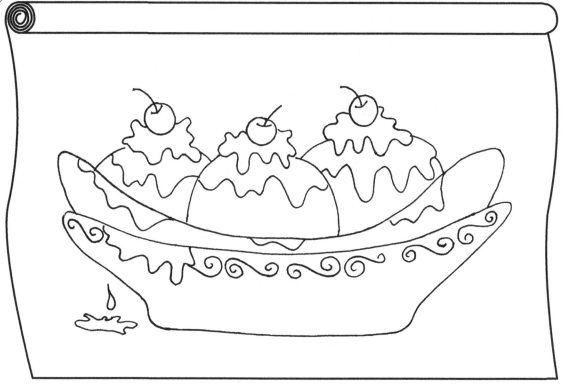

Plug it in!

Think about it and write it!

Can you think of **six adjectives** that describe the picture above? You may need to use a thesaurus.

❶ [_____]   ❹ [_____]

❷ [_____]   ❺ [_____]

❸ [_____]   ❻ [_____]

Dig in!

Write three sentences about the picture above using the six adjectives.

Color the picture.

❶ _____

_____

❷ _____

_____

❸ _____

_____

Plan the Design

Listen to the details of the story carefully!

On a separate piece of paper, draw what you hear as it is being read aloud to you.

In the Spotlight!

Highlight it!
Circle it!

Use a highlighter to identify **at least five adjectives**.

Then, with a pencil, **circle the noun** it describes.

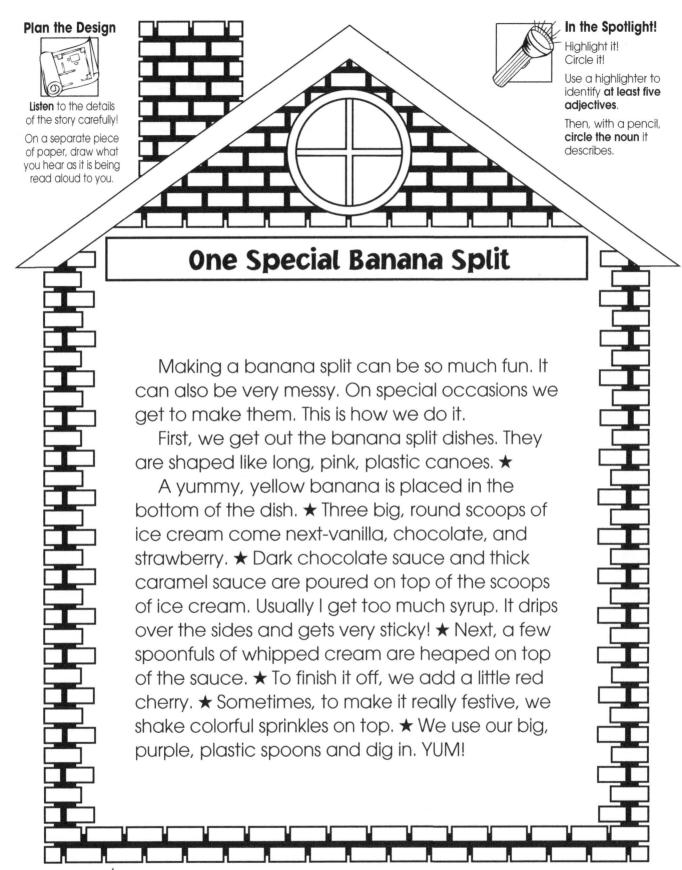

One Special Banana Split

Making a banana split can be so much fun. It can also be very messy. On special occasions we get to make them. This is how we do it.

First, we get out the banana split dishes. They are shaped like long, pink, plastic canoes. ★

A yummy, yellow banana is placed in the bottom of the dish. ★ Three big, round scoops of ice cream come next-vanilla, chocolate, and strawberry. ★ Dark chocolate sauce and thick caramel sauce are poured on top of the scoops of ice cream. Usually I get too much syrup. It drips over the sides and gets very sticky! ★ Next, a few spoonfuls of whipped cream are heaped on top of the sauce. ★ To finish it off, we add a little red cherry. ★ Sometimes, to make it really festive, we shake colorful sprinkles on top. ★ We use our big, purple, plastic spoons and dig in. YUM!

Tack it on!
Extend It!

Think of how a peanut butter and jelly sandwich, a hotdog, or a hamburger is made. Choose one of these and write in sequential order how it is made. Draw a picture.

Name: _____

Looking for Adjectives

**Check
the plans!**

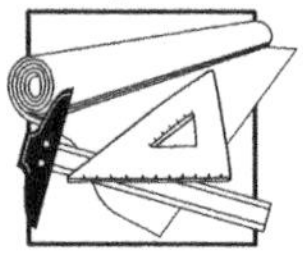

Study it!

What things do
you see? Look for
ALL of the details
in the illustration.

Plug it in!

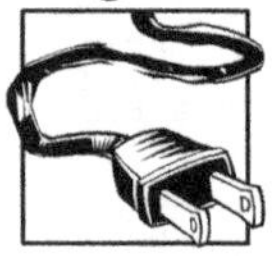

Think about it
and write it!

Can you think of **six adjectives** that describe the picture above? You may need to use a thesaurus.

1 _____   **4** _____

2 _____   **5** _____

3 _____   **6** _____

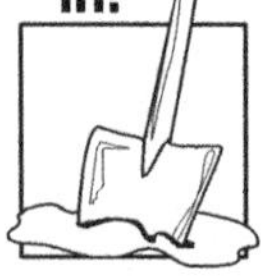

Write three
sentences about
the picture above
using the six
adjectives.

Color the picture.

1 _____

_____

2 _____

_____

3 _____

_____

Plan the Design

Listen to the details of the story carefully!

On a separate piece of paper, draw what you hear as it is being read aloud to you.

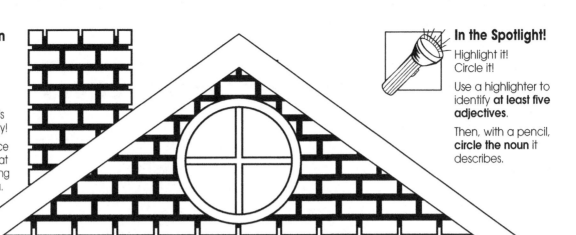

Sparkles the Clown

One of my favorite family memories is our trip to the circus. We saw many entertaining talents, the trapeze artists, the human cannonball, and several great animal shows.

I enjoyed watching the hilarious clown acts most of all! They all piled out of a tiny, pink car. Each clown began performing on a unicycle, a bicycle with one wheel. My favorite clown, Sparkles, was the funniest of all. His very round face was painted white. ★ He was wearing a tiny, striped, party hat with a large, purple pom-pom on top. ★ His wild, green, curly hair sprung from under his hat and spiraled around his jovial face. ★ Sparkles had a blue star around each eye and a large, red nose. ★ Of course, he was also wearing a gigantic smile! ★ A purple shirt, with polka dots in all the colors of the rainbow, covered his circle-shaped body. ★ His baggy pants had red and yellow stripes. He wore a pair of huge black shoes. ★ Sparkles was quite a colorful site to see!

I certainly enjoyed our family's trip to the circus. Maybe I will be a clown like Sparkles when I grow up.

Tack it on!

Extend It!

What is one of your favorite family memories? Were you on a vacation, celebrating a holiday, or just hanging around at home? Draw a picture of your special memory and write a paragraph about it.

Name: _____

Looking for Adjectives

Can you think of **six adjectives** that describe the picture above? You may need to use a thesaurus.

❶ _____   ❹ _____

❷ _____   ❺ _____

❸ _____   ❻ _____

❶ _____

_____

❷ _____

_____

❸ _____

_____

Plan the Design

Listen to the details of the story carefully!

On a separate piece of paper, draw what you hear as it is being read aloud to you.

Choo! Choo! Here Come the Bobcats!

Every fall season, Big City High School prepares for the homecoming celebration. Homecoming events encourage former students to return to the school for a visit.

The celebration at Big City High includes a football game, parade, cookout and school dance.

The cheerleaders were very excited about building a float for the homecoming parade, and decided to build a large train engine. They began building the float on a flat trailer with wheels, so it could roll along with the rest of the parade. ★ The body of the black engine was rectangular. ★ A small square sat on the top, left edge of the rectangle, representing the stately engineer's cabin. ★ A square-shaped opening was cut from the cabin, creating a window for the engineer to see. ★ A round, black pipe sat at the front of the engine's body, creating the train's tall smokestack. ★ The large, silver back wheels and small, silver front wheels made the big engine seem like it could roll down the tracks any minute! ★ A big, gold bell was attached to the body of the engine, in between the engineer's cabin and the smokestack. ★ A rope was attached to the bell, and when it was pulled, the shiny bell rang very loudly. ★

The ambitious cheerleaders rode on the creative float during the homecoming parade, happily cheering, "Roll right over the Panthers.... Go, Bobcats, Go! CHOO, CHOO!"

The enthusiastic crowd roared excitedly as the colorful floats rode by.

Tack it on!

Extend It!

Have you seen a parade? Have you ever watched a parade on TV? Draw a picture of your favorite parade float, or design your own. Describe it with five adjectives.

Name: _____

Looking for Adjectives

Check the plans!

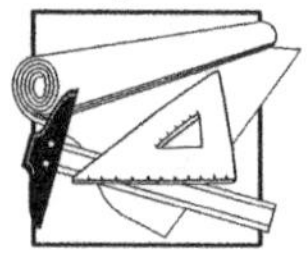

Study it!

What things do you see? Look for ALL of the details in the illustration.

- -

Plug it in!

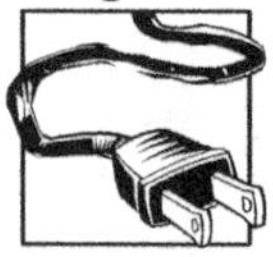

Think about it and write it!

Can you think of **six adjectives** that describe the picture above? You may need to use a thesaurus.

❶ _____   **❹** _____

❷ _____   **❺** _____

❸ _____   **❻** _____

- -

Dig in!

Write three sentences about the picture above using the six adjectives.

Color the picture.

❶ _____

_____

❷ _____

_____

❸ _____

_____

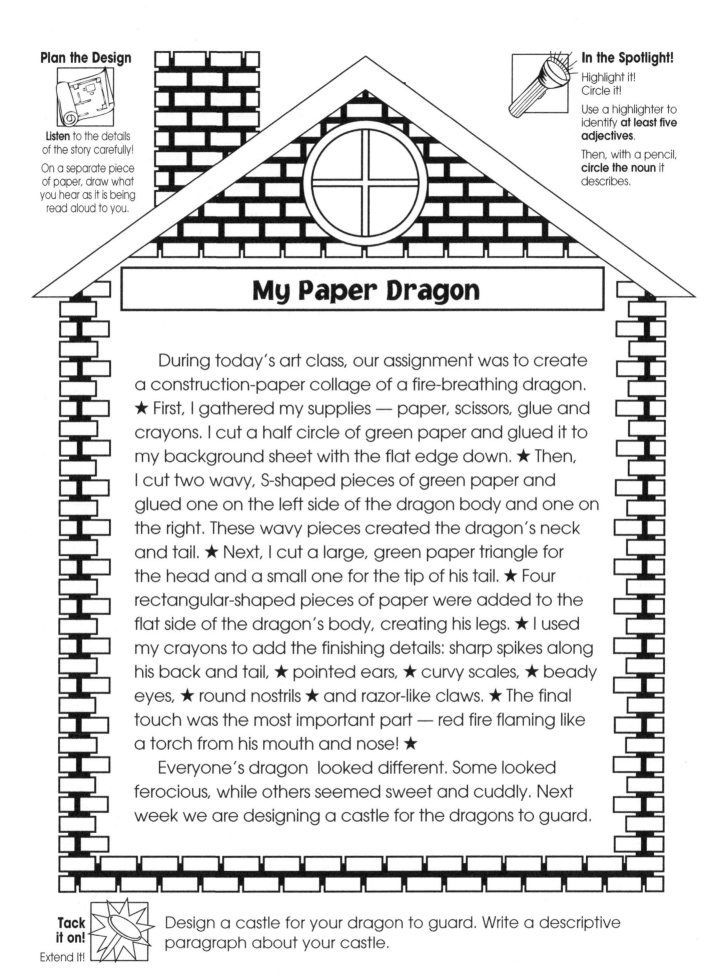

Listen to the details of the story carefully!

On a separate piece of paper, draw what you hear as it is being read aloud to you.

In the Spotlight!
Highlight it!
Circle it!

Use a highlighter to identify **at least five adjectives**.

Then, with a pencil, **circle the noun** it describes.

My Paper Dragon

During today's art class, our assignment was to create a construction-paper collage of a fire-breathing dragon. ★ First, I gathered my supplies — paper, scissors, glue and crayons. I cut a half circle of green paper and glued it to my background sheet with the flat edge down. ★ Then, I cut two wavy, S-shaped pieces of green paper and glued one on the left side of the dragon body and one on the right. These wavy pieces created the dragon's neck and tail. ★ Next, I cut a large, green paper triangle for the head and a small one for the tip of his tail. ★ Four rectangular-shaped pieces of paper were added to the flat side of the dragon's body, creating his legs. ★ I used my crayons to add the finishing details: sharp spikes along his back and tail, ★ pointed ears, ★ curvy scales, ★ beady eyes, ★ round nostrils ★ and razor-like claws. ★ The final touch was the most important part — red fire flaming like a torch from his mouth and nose! ★

Everyone's dragon looked different. Some looked ferocious, while others seemed sweet and cuddly. Next week we are designing a castle for the dragons to guard.

Tack it on!
Extend It!

Design a castle for your dragon to guard. Write a descriptive paragraph about your castle.

Name: _____

Looking for Adjectives

Check the plans!

Study it!

What things do you see? Look for ALL of the details in the illustration.

Plug it in!

Think about it and write it!

Can you think of **six adjectives** that describe the picture above? You may need to use a thesaurus.

❶ _____   ❹ _____

❷ _____   ❺ _____

❸ _____   ❻ _____

Dig in!

Write three sentences about the picture above using the six adjectives.

Color the picture.

❶ _____

_____

❷ _____

_____

❸ _____

_____

Plan the Design

Listen to the details of the story carefully!

On a separate piece of paper, draw what you hear as it is being read aloud to you.

Mortie's Adventurous Dream

Mortie Mouse was all tucked in his bed for a good night's sleep. He began reading his favorite bedtime story, "The Adventures of Titus the Mouse". As Mortie was reading, he started drifting off to sleep. He began to dream about a new adventure for Titus. In the dream, Titus was dressed in long khaki shorts and an orange shirt with two pockets. ★ He had a coiled rope tied on to his belt loop, and wore a sturdy pair of hiking boots. ★

Titus was standing at the base of a large, triangular shaped mountain made of cheese. ★ The bottom part of the mountain was made of mozzarella cheese; silky soft and a beautiful creamy color. ★ The middle section of the mountain was cheddar cheese; orange in color with a crumbly texture. ★ Swiss cheese created the mountain top; a soft, yellow cheese with lots of holes. ★ He climbed the mountain, snacking on chunks of cheese along the way.

As Titus reached the mountain top, Mortie awoke from his dream. His stomach was growling and he had a curious craving for a bite of Swiss cheese!

Tack it on!

Extend It!

Describe your food-related dream. What would the food be? What would you do with the food in your dream? Write about it.

Name: _____

Looking for Adjectives

Check the plans!

Study it!

What things do you see? Look for ALL of the details in the illustration.

- -

Plug it in!

Think about it and write it!

Can you think of **six adjectives** that describe the picture above? You may need to use a thesaurus.

❶ _____ ❹ _____

❷ _____ ❺ _____

❸ _____ ❻ _____

- -

Dig in!

Write three sentences about the picture above using the six adjectives.

Color the picture.

❶ _____

_____

❷ _____

_____

❸ _____

_____

Plan the Design

Listen to the details of the story carefully!

On a separate piece of paper, draw what you hear as it is being read aloud to you.

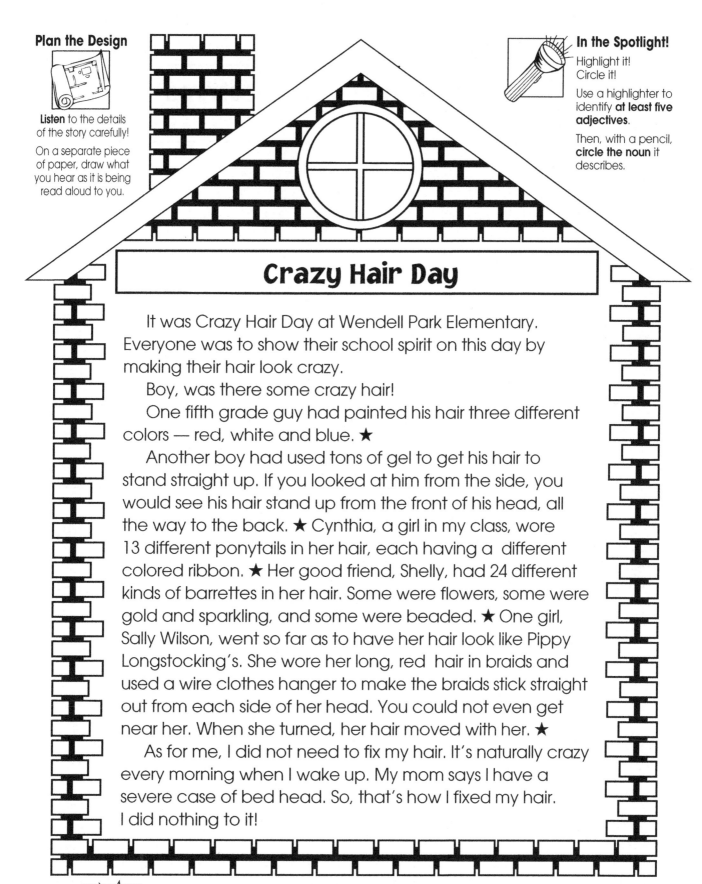

Crazy Hair Day

It was Crazy Hair Day at Wendell Park Elementary. Everyone was to show their school spirit on this day by making their hair look crazy.

Boy, was there some crazy hair!

One fifth grade guy had painted his hair three different colors — red, white and blue. ★

Another boy had used tons of gel to get his hair to stand straight up. If you looked at him from the side, you would see his hair stand up from the front of his head, all the way to the back. ★ Cynthia, a girl in my class, wore 13 different ponytails in her hair, each having a different colored ribbon. ★ Her good friend, Shelly, had 24 different kinds of barrettes in her hair. Some were flowers, some were gold and sparkling, and some were beaded. ★ One girl, Sally Wilson, went so far as to have her hair look like Pippy Longstocking's. She wore her long, red hair in braids and used a wire clothes hanger to make the braids stick straight out from each side of her head. You could not even get near her. When she turned, her hair moved with her. ★

As for me, I did not need to fix my hair. It's naturally crazy every morning when I wake up. My mom says I have a severe case of bed head. So, that's how I fixed my hair. I did nothing to it!

Tack it on!

Extend It!

Using a photograph, cut out your face and tape it to a piece of paper. Create crazy hair by using colored pencils and/or markers. Write a descriptive paragraph about you and your crazy hair.

Name: _____

Looking for Adjectives

Check the plans!

Study it!

What things do you see? Look for ALL of the details in the illustration.

Plug it in!

Think about it and write it!

Can you think of **six adjectives** that describe the picture above? You may need to use a thesaurus.

❶ _____   ❹ _____

❷ _____   ❺ _____

❸ _____   ❻ _____

Dig in!

Write three sentences about the picture above using the six adjectives.

Color the picture.

❶ _____

_____

❷ _____

_____

❸ _____

_____

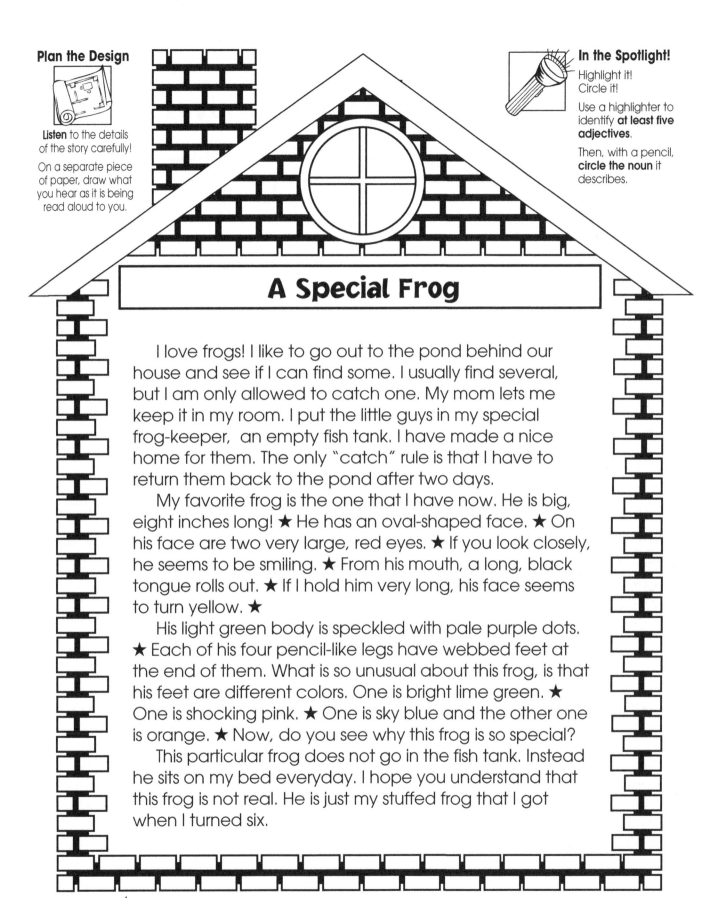

Listen to the details of the story carefully!

On a separate piece of paper, draw what you hear as it is being read aloud to you.

In the Spotlight!
Highlight it!
Circle it!

Use a highlighter to identify **at least five adjectives**.

Then, with a pencil, **circle the noun** it describes.

A Special Frog

I love frogs! I like to go out to the pond behind our house and see if I can find some. I usually find several, but I am only allowed to catch one. My mom lets me keep it in my room. I put the little guys in my special frog-keeper, an empty fish tank. I have made a nice home for them. The only "catch" rule is that I have to return them back to the pond after two days.

My favorite frog is the one that I have now. He is big, eight inches long! ★ He has an oval-shaped face. ★ On his face are two very large, red eyes. ★ If you look closely, he seems to be smiling. ★ From his mouth, a long, black tongue rolls out. ★ If I hold him very long, his face seems to turn yellow. ★

His light green body is speckled with pale purple dots. ★ Each of his four pencil-like legs have webbed feet at the end of them. What is so unusual about this frog, is that his feet are different colors. One is bright lime green. ★ One is shocking pink. ★ One is sky blue and the other one is orange. ★ Now, do you see why this frog is so special?

This particular frog does not go in the fish tank. Instead he sits on my bed everyday. I hope you understand that this frog is not real. He is just my stuffed frog that I got when I turned six.

Tack it on!
Extend It!

Do you have a favorite stuffed animal? Draw a picture of it and write a descriptive paragraph about it.

Name: _____

Looking for Adjectives

Check the plans!

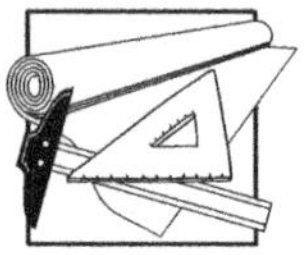

Study it!

What things do you see? Look for ALL of the details in the illustration.

Plug it in!

Think about it and write it!

Can you think of **six adjectives** that describe the picture above? You may need to use a thesaurus.

❶ _____   ❹ _____

❷ _____   ❺ _____

❸ _____   ❻ _____

Dig in!

Write three sentences about the picture above using the six adjectives.

Color the picture.

❶ _____

_____

❷ _____

_____

❸ _____

_____

Plan the Design

Listen to the details of the story carefully!

On a separate piece of paper, draw what you hear as it is being read aloud to you.

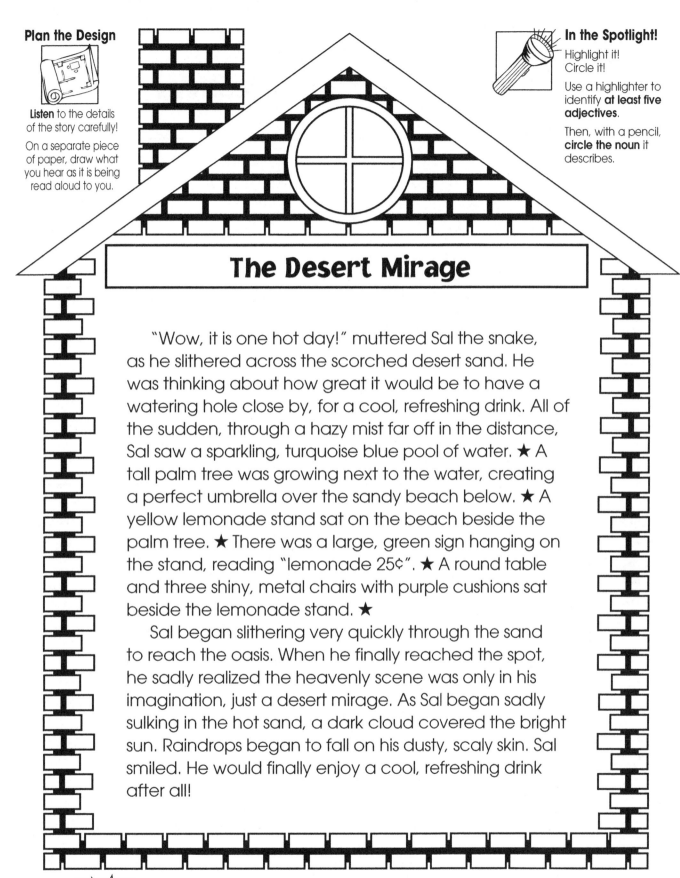

The Desert Mirage

"Wow, it is one hot day!" muttered Sal the snake, as he slithered across the scorched desert sand. He was thinking about how great it would be to have a watering hole close by, for a cool, refreshing drink. All of the sudden, through a hazy mist far off in the distance, Sal saw a sparkling, turquoise blue pool of water. ★ A tall palm tree was growing next to the water, creating a perfect umbrella over the sandy beach below. ★ A yellow lemonade stand sat on the beach beside the palm tree. ★ There was a large, green sign hanging on the stand, reading "lemonade 25¢". ★ A round table and three shiny, metal chairs with purple cushions sat beside the lemonade stand. ★

Sal began slithering very quickly through the sand to reach the oasis. When he finally reached the spot, he sadly realized the heavenly scene was only in his imagination, just a desert mirage. As Sal began sadly sulking in the hot sand, a dark cloud covered the bright sun. Raindrops began to fall on his dusty, scaly skin. Sal smiled. He would finally enjoy a cool, refreshing drink after all!

Tack it on!

Extend It!

Write a paragraph describing a memory of a hot, sunny day. Include what you did to get cool.

Name: _____

Looking for Adjectives

Check the plans!

Study it!

What things do you see? Look for ALL of the details in the illustration.

HARRY

- -

Plug it in!

Think about it and write it!

Can you think of **six adjectives** that describe the picture above? You may need to use a thesaurus.

❶ [   ]   ❹ [   ]

❷ [   ]   ❺ [   ]

❸ [   ]   ❻ [   ]

- -

Dig in!

Write three sentences about the picture above using the six adjectives.

Color the picture.

❶ _____

_____

❷ _____

_____

❸ _____

_____

Plan the Design

Listen to the details of the story carefully!

On a separate piece of paper, draw what you hear as it is being read aloud to you.

The Best Dogs in America

Dogs! I love them! We have three of them, Henry, Boomer, and Biscuit. I think they are the best dogs in America! I know, everyone thinks their dog is the best. But let me tell you about my dogs.

Henry is very little. He is part Chihuahua and part Maltese. ★ His face looks like a Chihuahua with a pointed nose, ★ tiny eyes, ★ and little stand-up ears. ★ He has a white, furry body. He looks like a little fat snowball. ★ His tail is short and fluffy. ★ The best thing about Henry is that he sleeps with me.

Boomer is a greyhound. He is very tall and slender with not much fur at all. ★ He has extremely long legs. ★ A long nose protrudes from his face along with short black whiskers. ★ His ears are small and floppy. When he hears noise, they stand up at attention like a soldier. ★ His long, spotted tail wags very quickly when he hears noise. ★ Boomer is light brown. ★ The best thing about Boomer is that he can run faster than lightning!

Biscuit is our two-year-old cocker spaniel. He is a medium-sized dog. ★ He has long white hair on his legs and his paws. ★ The hair on his back is very short. Half way down his sides, white and brown-spotted hair drags the floor. We have to brush Biscuit often. His little, furry tail wags all the time. ★ He has long brown ears, ★ big black eyes, ★ and a spotted nose. ★ The best thing about Biscuit is that he plays with me and my friends all the time.

Now you know why I think my dogs are the best dogs in America!

Tack it on!

Extend It!

Write a description of your dog or one you would like to have. Read your description to a friend and have them draw your dog.

Name: _____

Looking for Adjectives

Check the plans!

Study it!

What things do you see? Look for ALL of the details in the illustration.

· ·

Plug it in!

Think about it and write it!

Can you think of **six adjectives** that describe the picture above? You may need to use a thesaurus.

❶    ❹

❷ _____   ❺ _____

❸ _____   ❻ _____

· ·

Dig in!

Write three sentences about the picture above using the six adjectives.

Color the picture.

❶ _____

_____

❷ _____

_____

❸ _____

_____

Plan the Design

Listen to the details of the story carefully!

On a separate piece of paper, draw what you hear as it is being read aloud to you.

In the Spotlight!

Highlight it!
Circle it!

Use a highlighter to identify **at least five adjectives**.

Then, with a pencil, **circle the noun** it describes.

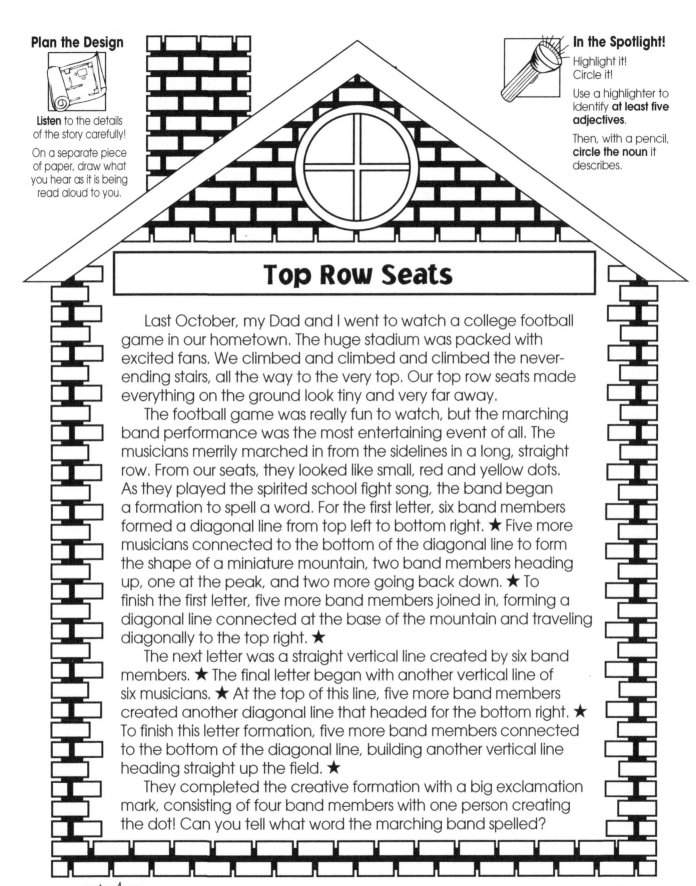

Top Row Seats

Last October, my Dad and I went to watch a college football game in our hometown. The huge stadium was packed with excited fans. We climbed and climbed and climbed the never-ending stairs, all the way to the very top. Our top row seats made everything on the ground look tiny and very far away.

The football game was really fun to watch, but the marching band performance was the most entertaining event of all. The musicians merrily marched in from the sidelines in a long, straight row. From our seats, they looked like small, red and yellow dots. As they played the spirited school fight song, the band began a formation to spell a word. For the first letter, six band members formed a diagonal line from top left to bottom right. ★ Five more musicians connected to the bottom of the diagonal line to form the shape of a miniature mountain, two band members heading up, one at the peak, and two more going back down. ★ To finish the first letter, five more band members joined in, forming a diagonal line connected at the base of the mountain and traveling diagonally to the top right. ★

The next letter was a straight vertical line created by six band members. ★ The final letter began with another vertical line of six musicians. ★ At the top of this line, five more band members created another diagonal line that headed for the bottom right. ★ To finish this letter formation, five more band members connected to the bottom of the diagonal line, building another vertical line heading straight up the field. ★

They completed the creative formation with a big exclamation mark, consisting of four band members with one person creating the dot! Can you tell what word the marching band spelled?

Tack it on!

Extend It!

Create a fun strumming instrument with an empty tissue box and a few rubber bands. Using rubber bands in a variety of sizes, put a few around the box overlapping the opening. Pluck the bands, and you will be surprised at the great tones you can make!

Name: _____

Looking for Adjectives

....

Plug it in!

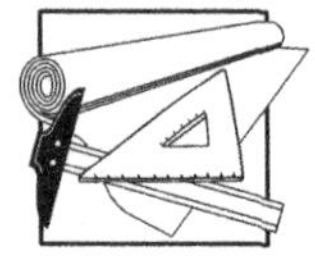

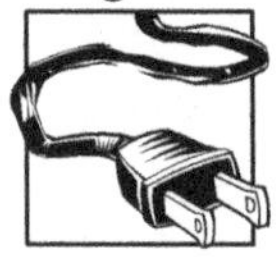

Think about it and write it!

Can you think of **six adjectives** that describe the picture above? You may need to use a thesaurus.

❶ _____   ❹ _____

❷ _____   ❺ _____

❸ _____   ❻ _____

....

Dig in!

Write three sentences about the picture above using the six adjectives.

Color the picture.

❶ _____

_____

❷ _____

_____

❸ _____

_____

Plan the Design

Listen to the details of the story carefully!

On a separate piece of paper, draw what you hear as it is being read aloud to you.

In the Spotlight!

Highlight it!
Circle it!

Use a highlighter to identify **at least five adjectives**.

Then, with a pencil, **circle the noun** it describes.

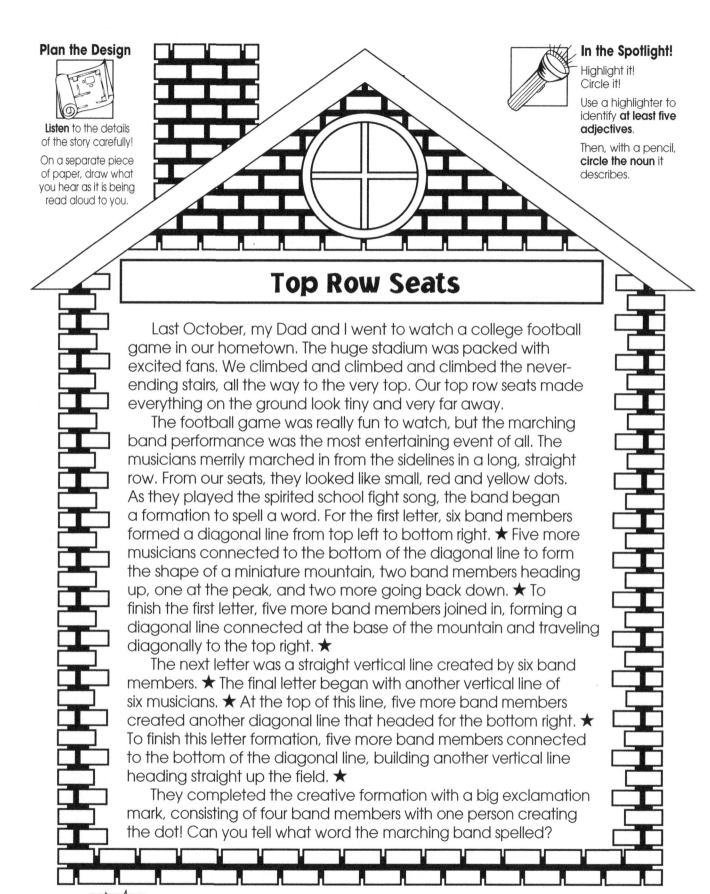

Top Row Seats

Last October, my Dad and I went to watch a college football game in our hometown. The huge stadium was packed with excited fans. We climbed and climbed and climbed the never-ending stairs, all the way to the very top. Our top row seats made everything on the ground look tiny and very far away.

The football game was really fun to watch, but the marching band performance was the most entertaining event of all. The musicians merrily marched in from the sidelines in a long, straight row. From our seats, they looked like small, red and yellow dots. As they played the spirited school fight song, the band began a formation to spell a word. For the first letter, six band members formed a diagonal line from top left to bottom right. ★ Five more musicians connected to the bottom of the diagonal line to form the shape of a miniature mountain, two band members heading up, one at the peak, and two more going back down. ★ To finish the first letter, five more band members joined in, forming a diagonal line connected at the base of the mountain and traveling diagonally to the top right. ★

The next letter was a straight vertical line created by six band members. ★ The final letter began with another vertical line of six musicians. ★ At the top of this line, five more band members created another diagonal line that headed for the bottom right. ★ To finish this letter formation, five more band members connected to the bottom of the diagonal line, building another vertical line heading straight up the field. ★

They completed the creative formation with a big exclamation mark, consisting of four band members with one person creating the dot! Can you tell what word the marching band spelled?

Tack it on!

Extend It!

Create a fun strumming instrument with an empty tissue box and a few rubber bands. Using rubber bands in a variety of sizes, put a few around the box overlapping the opening. Pluck the bands, and you will be surprised at the great tones you can make!

Name: _____

Looking for Adjectives

Can you think of **six adjectives** that describe the picture above? You may need to use a thesaurus.

1 _____   **4** _____

2 _____   **5** _____

3 _____   **6** _____

1 _____

_____

2 _____

_____

3 _____

_____

Plan the Design

Listen to the details of the story carefully!

On a separate piece of paper, draw what you hear as it is being read aloud to you.

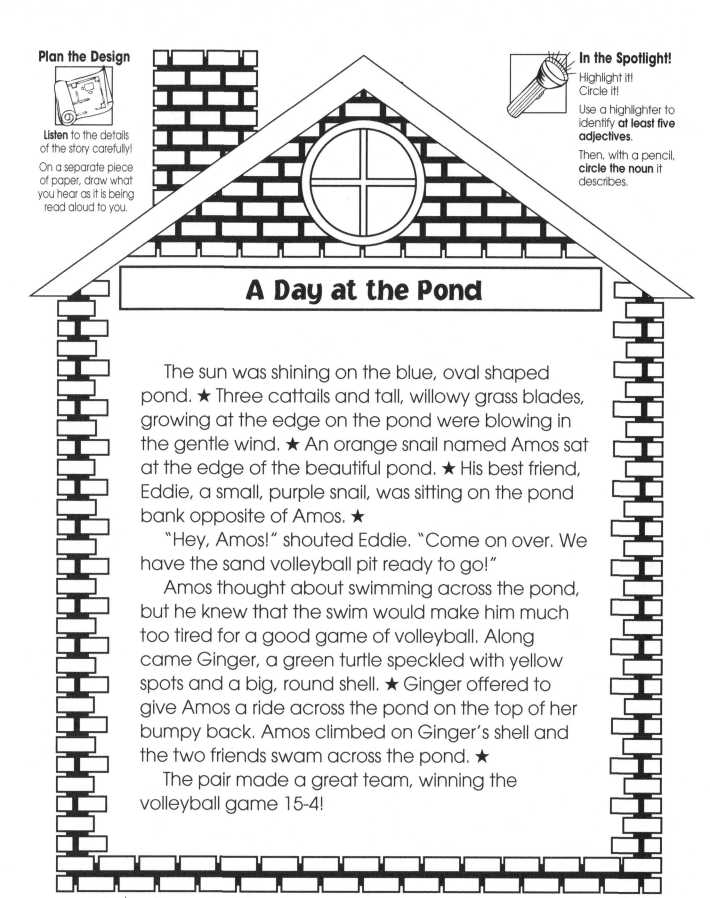

A Day at the Pond

The sun was shining on the blue, oval shaped pond. ★ Three cattails and tall, willowy grass blades, growing at the edge on the pond were blowing in the gentle wind. ★ An orange snail named Amos sat at the edge of the beautiful pond. ★ His best friend, Eddie, a small, purple snail, was sitting on the pond bank opposite of Amos. ★

"Hey, Amos!" shouted Eddie. "Come on over. We have the sand volleyball pit ready to go!"

Amos thought about swimming across the pond, but he knew that the swim would make him much too tired for a good game of volleyball. Along came Ginger, a green turtle speckled with yellow spots and a big, round shell. ★ Ginger offered to give Amos a ride across the pond on the top of her bumpy back. Amos climbed on Ginger's shell and the two friends swam across the pond. ★

The pair made a great team, winning the volleyball game 15-4!

Tack it on!

Extend It!

Create three new characters that might hang out at the pond. What activities do they enjoy? Draw a picture of the new pond friends and write a paragraph about them.

Name: _____

Looking for Adjectives

Check the plans!

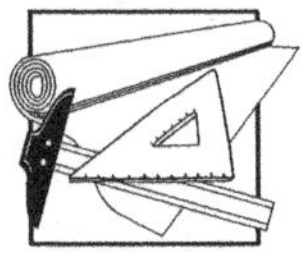

Study it!

What things do you see? Look for ALL of the details in the illustration.

Plug it in!

Think about it and write it!

Can you think of **six adjectives** that describe the picture above? You may need to use a thesaurus.

❶ _____   ❹ _____

❷ _____   ❺ _____

❸ _____   ❻ _____

Dig in!

Write three sentences about the picture above using the six adjectives.

Color the picture.

❶ _____

_____

❷ _____

_____

❸ _____

_____

Plan the Design

Listen to the details of the story carefully!

On a separate piece of paper, draw what you hear as it is being read aloud to you.

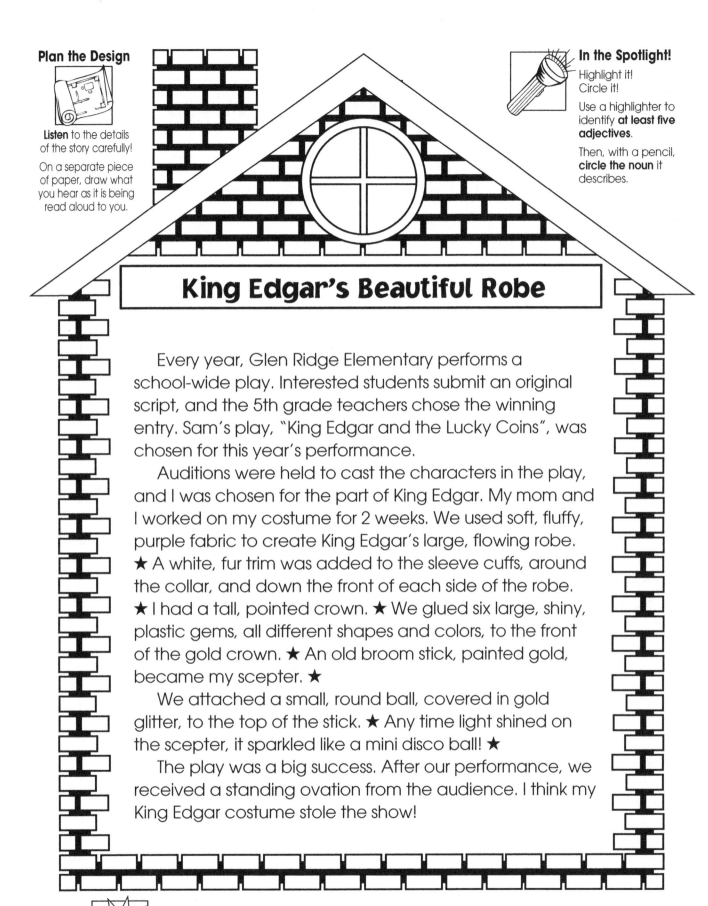

King Edgar's Beautiful Robe

Every year, Glen Ridge Elementary performs a school-wide play. Interested students submit an original script, and the 5th grade teachers chose the winning entry. Sam's play, "King Edgar and the Lucky Coins", was chosen for this year's performance.

Auditions were held to cast the characters in the play, and I was chosen for the part of King Edgar. My mom and I worked on my costume for 2 weeks. We used soft, fluffy, purple fabric to create King Edgar's large, flowing robe. ★ A white, fur trim was added to the sleeve cuffs, around the collar, and down the front of each side of the robe. ★ I had a tall, pointed crown. ★ We glued six large, shiny, plastic gems, all different shapes and colors, to the front of the gold crown. ★ An old broom stick, painted gold, became my scepter. ★

We attached a small, round ball, covered in gold glitter, to the top of the stick. ★ Any time light shined on the scepter, it sparkled like a mini disco ball! ★

The play was a big success. After our performance, we received a standing ovation from the audience. I think my King Edgar costume stole the show!

Tack it on!

Extend It!

Make a paper crown and decorate it. Write a descriptive paragraph about the crown.

Name: _____

Looking for Adjectives

Check the plans!

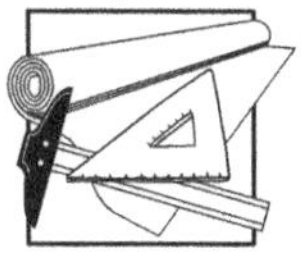

Study it!

What things do you see? Look for ALL of the details in the illustration.

Plug it in!

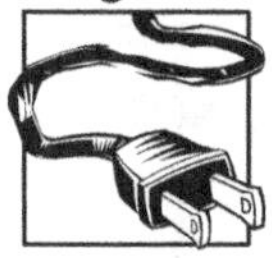

Think about it and write it!

Can you think of **six adjectives** that describe the picture above? You may need to use a thesaurus.

❶ _____   ❹ _____

❷ _____   ❺ _____

❸ _____   ❻ _____

Dig in!

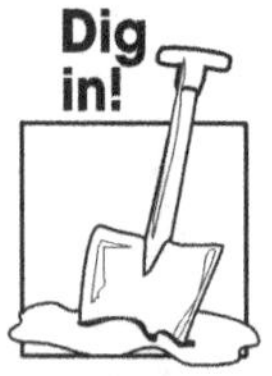

Write three sentences about the picture above using the six adjectives.

Color the picture.

❶ _____

_____

❷ _____

_____

❸ _____

_____

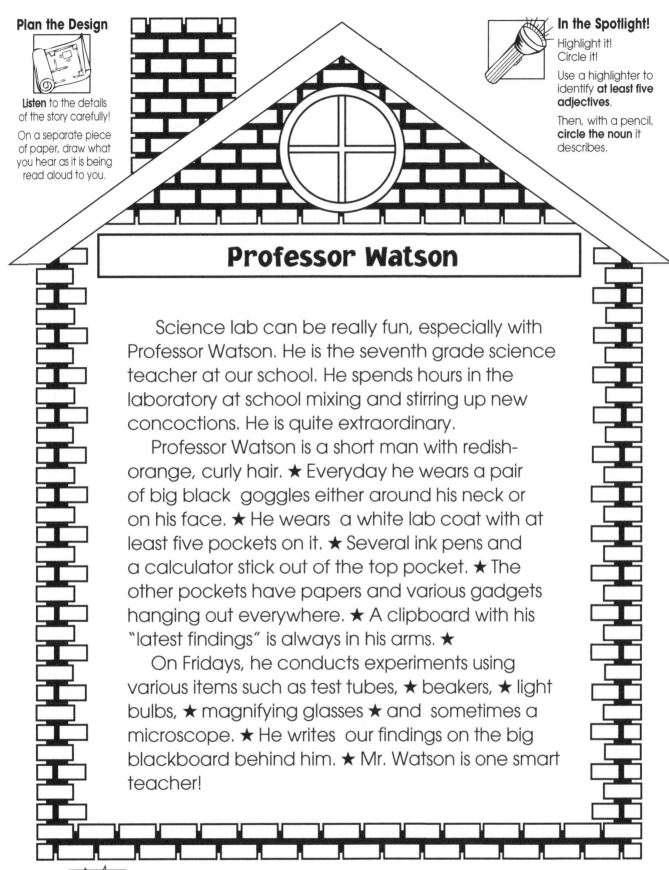

Plan the Design

Listen to the details of the story carefully!

On a separate piece of paper, draw what you hear as it is being read aloud to you.

In the Spotlight!

Highlight it!
Circle it!

Use a highlighter to identify **at least five adjectives**.

Then, with a pencil, **circle the noun** it describes.

Professor Watson

Science lab can be really fun, especially with Professor Watson. He is the seventh grade science teacher at our school. He spends hours in the laboratory at school mixing and stirring up new concoctions. He is quite extraordinary.

Professor Watson is a short man with redish-orange, curly hair. ★ Everyday he wears a pair of big black goggles either around his neck or on his face. ★ He wears a white lab coat with at least five pockets on it. ★ Several ink pens and a calculator stick out of the top pocket. ★ The other pockets have papers and various gadgets hanging out everywhere. ★ A clipboard with his "latest findings" is always in his arms. ★

On Fridays, he conducts experiments using various items such as test tubes, ★ beakers, ★ light bulbs, ★ magnifying glasses ★ and sometimes a microscope. ★ He writes our findings on the big blackboard behind him. ★ Mr. Watson is one smart teacher!

Tack it on!
Extend It!

Conduct a simple experiment. Write down your findings.

Name: _____

Looking for Adjectives

Check the plans!

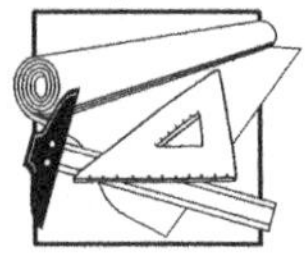

Study it!

What things do you see? Look for ALL of the details in the illustration.

Plug it in!

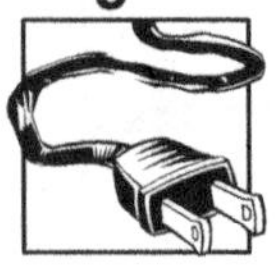

Think about it and write it!

Can you think of **six adjectives** that describe the picture above? You may need to use a thesaurus.

❶ _____   ❹ _____

❷ _____   ❺ _____

❸ _____   ❻ _____

Dig in!

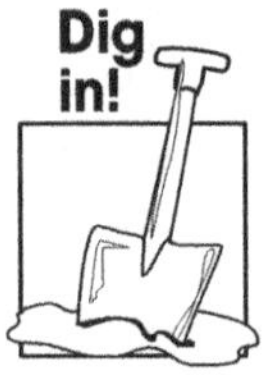

Write three sentences about the picture above using the six adjectives.

Color the picture.

❶ _____

❷ _____

_____

❸ _____

_____

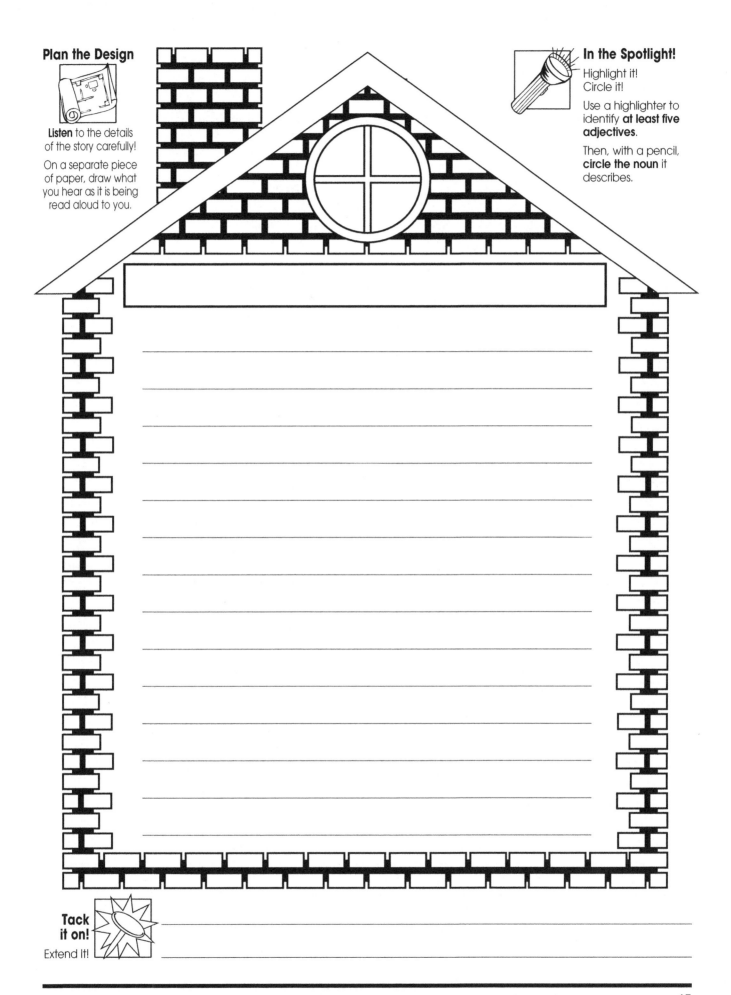

Plan the Design

Listen to the details of the story carefully!

On a separate piece of paper, draw what you hear as it is being read aloud to you.

In the Spotlight!

Highlight it!
Circle it!

Use a highlighter to identify **at least five adjectives**.

Then, with a pencil, **circle the noun** it describes.

Tack it on!

Extend It!

Read the three words in each row and circle the two adjectives.

Example: flower *(juicy)*

1. charming   young   run
2. fast   Sarah   jolly
3. hungry   apple   cool
4. sandwich   tight   new
5. tall   plain   dog

6. farm   gorgeous   yellow
7. small   kite   shiny
8. sharp   delicious   bag
9. bed   round   green
10. boy   icy   sunny

Write an adjective to describe each of the nouns below.
*Example: **messy** pig*

1. _____ car
2. _____ pencil
3. _____ telephone
4. _____ ball
5. _____ quilt

6. _____ fire
7. _____ trash
8. _____ turtle
9. _____ box
10. _____ smile

Write a sentence using ONE adjective.

1. _____

Write a sentence using TWO adjectives.

2. _____

Write a sentence using THREE adjectives.

3. _____

Circle the adjectives in the sentences below.

1. The loud girls cheered as the football team ran through the big sign.

2. We saw the speeding car go down the rocky road.

3. Five yellow flowers were growing next to the tall tree.

4. The fire-breathing dragon scared the lovely princess.

5. The funny clowns rode little bikes around the big ring.

6. Mom bakes delicious cherry pies .

7. Tiny mice were eating chunks of yellow cheese.

8. Our big snowman melted quickly from the hot, shining sun.

9. Eight orange pumpkins were delivered on my grandma's front steps.

10. Nick found his striped, wool sweater on the dirty floor.

Directions: Write an adjective in each blank that begins with that particular letter.

1. j _____

2. b _____

3. t _____

4. a _____

5. p _____

6. h _____

7. s _____

8. g _____

9. f _____

10. e _____

More Adjective Words

Note: Use the templates on pages 44-45 for creating more activities. Also, use these words with the Adjective Fun Sheet activity on page 50.

adventurous	delicious	horrible
angry	dizzy	hungry
artistic	dry	itchy
athletic	dull	jittery
bad	enormous	jolly
better	excited	juicy
beautiful	fair	kind
big	fat	lazy
black	far	little
blond	frail	long
bright	friendly	loud
charming	funny	magnificent
chewy	fuzzy	magenta
circular	generous	many
clean	great	mighty
clever	green	mushy
clumsy	gigantic	musical
cool	gorgeous	nasty
crazy	grumpy	naughty
crunchy	handsome	new
curly	happy	nice

Reading FUNdamentals™ — Adjectives ©2016 www.barkercreek.com

More Adjective Words

Note: Use the templates on pages 44-45 for creating more activities. Also, use these words with the Adjective Fun Sheet activity on page 50.

nosy	sad	tan
nutty	salty	tart
nutritious	scary	thick
odd	selfish	thin
old	shiny	timid
outgoing	short	tender
orange	shy	tricky
ordinary	silly	tough
plain	skinny	ugly
plump	small	unique
prickly	smooth	unpleasant
pretty	speckled	vast
precious	spotty	various
proud	sticky	versatile
purple	strange	wasteful
quiet	striped	wild
quick	stubborn	wonderful
rainy	square	yellow
red	sweet	young
rough	talented	yummy
round	tall	zany

Adjective Fun Sheet

Directions:
Choose two adjectives from the adjectives word list. Next, think of a picture that would demonstrate these two adjectives. Write a sentence that tells about your picture. **Note**: *Some sentences may get really crazy!*

Here is something

_____
(adjective)

and

_____ .
(adjective)

It is a_____

_____

. . . .

Adjective Fun Sheet

Name: _____

Directions:
Choose two adjectives from the adjectives word list. Next, think of a picture that would demonstrate these two adjectives. Write a sentence that tells about your picture. **Note**: *Some sentences may get really crazy!*

Here is something

_____
(adjective)

and

_____ .
(adjective)

It is a_____

_____

Made in the USA
Middletown, DE
31 March 2022

63445604R00031